THE
12
LAWS
OF

BY KEITH WELBORN

THE
12 LAWS
OF
DJING

BY KEITH WELBORN

ISBN 979-8-9878760-2-2
Publisher: Keybo Entertainment
8549 Wilshire Blvd #2343
Beverly Hills, CA 90212
www.keyboent.com

Excerpt From
The 12 Laws of DJing

To my father, the man who got me into the mix.

Love you, Pops.

—Grasshopper

"WORK IT, MAKE IT, DO IT, MAKES US HARDER, BETTER, FASTER, STRONGER."
– DAFT PUNK

So, you want to be a DJ?

You want to control the energy of the room. You want to make the crowd move, command the decks with precision, and leave people talking about your set long after the night is over. You want the bookings, the status, the respect, and yeah—the money that comes with it.

That's dope. But let's be real.

If your only goal is to press play and cash a check, you might as well put this book down now. DJing isn't just about blending tracks—it's an art, a science, and a culture. Somewhere along the way, the fundamentals got lost, buried under convenience and the rise of plug-and-play DJs who barely scratch the surface of what this craft truly is.

This book is here to change that.

I'm here to take you back to the essence—to the foundation that separates real DJs from button mashers. You're not just playing music. You're orchestrating an experience. You're crafting a moment. You're conducting the rhythm of the night.

And that doesn't happen by accident. It happens by following the 12 Laws of DJing—the essential principles that every real DJ must live by.

Why Most DJs Fall Short

Too many DJs think pressing play is enough. Technology has made it so easy to DJ that people skip the fundamentals entirely. And the crowd? They don't always know the difference—at least, not at first.

The Problem?
•Too many DJs are just playing songs, not controlling the room.
•Technology has made DJing too easy, letting people skip real skill.
•The crowd often sees DJs as button pushers, not artists.

And that's a problem.

Because when people think anyone can do this, the craft loses its respect. And when that happens, the real DJs—the ones who actually care, who practice, who put in the work—get lumped in with the ones who are just chasing clout.

I don't like that for us.

The craft deserves better. And it's up to real DJs to take it back.

Who Am I to Teach You?

I'll keep it one hundred with you—I am NOT the best DJ in the world. Not even close.

I'm just a guy who started DJing at 12 years old, messing around with my dad's setup, and never stopped.

✔ 20+ years in the game
✔ Trained with some of the best
✔ Traveled the world & made great money
✔ Rocked thousands of crowds

And through it all, I've seen the shift. Some DJs stepped up and mastered their craft. Others got lazy, relying on sync buttons and pre-recorded sets. I've watched talented DJs get overlooked while flashier, clout-chasing ones took center stage.

That's why I wrote this book.

Because the DJs who take shortcuts won't last. And the ones who take this seriously? They get booked for decades.

You cannot become a great DJ without mastering the fundamentals.

Think about sports:
    •Basketball players need proper footwork, shooting form, and defense.
    •Boxers need precise technique, speed, and power.
    •Musicians need rhythm, timing, and control.

And DJs?
    •Beatmatching – If your mix isn't tight, nothing else matters.
    •Blending & Transitions – Creating a seamless flow keeps the energy locked in.
    •EQ Control & Sound Manipulation – Knowing how to shape the sound makes or breaks a set.
    •Crowd Reading & Engagement – The ability to read the room and adjust is what separates DJs from playlist curators.

A DJ who masters these skills doesn't just play music —they create moments. They command a space. They control emotions.

This book is your roadmap to DJ mastery. By the time you finish, I want you to be:
    ✔ In high demand
    ✔ Respected by your peers
    ✔ A true crowd controller

Because let's be honest—owning DJ gear doesn't make you a DJ, just like owning a basketball doesn't make you an athlete.

If you're ready to:
✔ Step up and put in the work
✔ Challenge yourself to be better
✔ Elevate your craft and stand out

Then let's go.

MIX ON BEAT.

"Rhythm is the beauty of life. It is the energy that excites and drives us to move forward."
—Herbie Hancock

ACT'N A FOOL

The Power of Rhythm: The DJ's Secret Weapon

Ever been deep in the groove, fully locked into a song, feeling every beat—only to be yanked out of it by a sloppy transition or an awkward tempo shift? That split second of disconnection kills the vibe, shatters the energy, and can turn an electrified dance floor into a confused mess.

Rhythm is everything.

The word itself comes from the Ancient Greek rhythmos, meaning a steady, repeated motion, and rhein, meaning to flow. Just like a human heartbeat keeps a steady rhythm—where any irregularity can be serious—the same applies to music. As a DJ, your job is to maintain the pulse of the party.

You're not just playing songs. You're conducting an orchestra of movement, emotion, and anticipation.

A skilled DJ doesn't just understand rhythm—they command it. A sudden, unintentional tempo shift can break the mood, throw off dancers, and leave the crowd disconnected. DJing isn't about playing two songs back-to-back—it's about seamlessly fusing them into one fluid, hypnotic experience.

To master rhythm like a pro, you need to:

✔ Recognize beats and timing – Know when to drop, when to build, and when to let a track breathe.

✔ Maintain a steady tempo – Keeping the energy consistent ensures no one stumbles out of the groove.

✔ Blend transitions seamlessly – The art of a clean mix is what separates professionals from amateurs.

Rhythm isn't just a skill—it's your foundation.

The best DJs aren't just selectors, they're conductors of energy. They understand that when rhythm is consistent, the crowd stays locked in, the dance floor stays moving, and the night becomes legendary.

If you master rhythm, you don't just play music—you control the pulse of the room.

THE BLUEPRINT

The Art of Mixing on Beat: Precision, Flow, and Control

Mixing on beat is what separates a hypnotic, immersive DJ set from one that feels clunky, disconnected, and amateur. A great DJ doesn't just play tracks—they weave a seamless sonic journey that keeps the crowd engaged from the first drop to the final encore.

Think of a DJ set like a marathon—long, steady, and full of energy. When done right, the transitions are invisible. The audience isn't thinking about the mix; they're feeling it, locked into the groove without ever questioning how the rhythm is being maintained.

But here's the truth: One sloppy transition can destroy that magic in an instant.

A single off-beat mix can snap a crowd out of their trance, disrupting the momentum and killing the energy. And it doesn't matter if the partygoers don't have a trained ear—they can feel it when something is off. A DJ who can't mix on beat isn't just making a technical mistake—they're committing a cardinal sin against the dancefloor.

Understanding Song Structure: The Blueprint for Smooth Transitions

A true DJ isn't just familiar with music—they understand it. To mix effectively, you need to know how songs are structured. Every track is built from distinct sections:

-Introduction – The lead-in, often instrumental, setting up the vibe.
- Verse – The storytelling or lyrical section that drives the song forward.
-Chorus (Hook) – The high-energy centerpiece of the track, the part everyone remembers.
-Bridge – A transitional moment that breaks up repetition before returning to the hook.

These sections are divided into counted beats and phrases, usually grouped in patterns of 4, 8, 16, or 32. Recognizing these patterns is what allows a DJ to time their transitions perfectly and keep the energy flowing without a hitch.

Timing Your Transitions: The Science of a Seamless Blend

A pro-level DJ always matches the measure count between tracks. Here's how:

If you're transitioning into a song's first chorus at a 16-count structure, the incoming track should debut at its own hook or verse within the same 16-count window—creating a natural flow.

Alternatively, you can divide a verse in half and introduce the new track midway through a 32-beat phrase, keeping the rhythm locked.

For beginners, mixing "on the one" (starting the next track precisely on the first beat of a new phrase) is a great way to build timing and accuracy. This ensures that every blend feels natural and intentional, rather than random or forced.

Maintaining Rhythm & Key: The Golden Rule of Mixing

A DJ's greatest weapon is rhythm. If you can keep the beats aligned, the energy never drops. But rhythm alone isn't enough—key matters, too.

If two tracks clash in key, even a perfectly timed transition can feel off, creating unwanted tension in the mix. To avoid this:

• Use harmonic mixing techniques—match songs that share a compatible key or shift keys gradually.
• Keep a close ear on basslines—if they don't blend smoothly, they'll make the transition sound muddy.
• Rely on EQ adjustments—subtle tweaks in highs, mids, and lows can keep everything feeling cohesive.

The Mark of a True DJ: Effortless Control

At its core, mixing on beat isn't just a skill—it's an art. A great DJ doesn't just play music—they control the energy of the room, keeping the crowd in a state of rhythm-induced hypnosis.

Master this, and you won't just be another DJ.

You'll be the one they talk about.

If you fail to do so, your audience is likely to notice, as music is a universal language that can be understood and appreciated by people from all cultures.

The Unbreakable Law: Mixing on Beat

Once you've mastered counting beats and breaking down song structures, a whole new world of possibilities opens up. You'll be able to push past the basics and experiment with scratching, sampling, and beat juggling —techniques that separate DJs from human playlists. These elements add creativity, style, and signature flair to your sets, giving you the edge over the competition.

But let's get one thing straight: None of that matters if you can't mix on beat.

Mixing on beat is not optional—it's the law.

I'll say it louder for the DJs in the back: You cannot call yourself a DJ if you can't mix to the beat.

This is the foundation of everything you do behind the decks. Without rhythm, your transitions will be sloppy, your blends will feel forced, and your audience—whether they realize it or not—will feel the disconnect.

Even if a partygoer can't explain why something sounds off, they can feel it. And if the energy drops because of a bad mix? You've lost them.

Rhythm Can't Be Taught—But It Can Be Learned

I'll keep it real with you—teaching rhythm through words on a page is tough. You can read about beat counting, phrasing, and transitions all day, but until you hear it, feel it, and practice it, it won't fully click.

So, if you're struggling with timing, beat counting, or locking in that perfect mix—don't trip.

I've got you covered.

Check out my YouTube channel, where I break it all down visually and in detail, showing you exactly how to recognize beats, count phrases, and mix like a pro. Seeing and hearing these techniques in action will help you lock them into muscle memory.

Because in this game, rhythm isn't just a skill. It's your lifeline.

THE FLIP SIDE

The Art of the Drop: When to Let the Beat Breathe

Mixing on beat and in key is essential in genres like house and techno, where smooth transitions define the experience. But when it comes to hip-hop, open format, and party DJing, the rules shift…kinda. Perfection in blending isn't always the goal—sometimes, the most electrifying moment comes from dropping a track exactly when it needs to hit.

A well-placed drop isn't just about song selection—it's about timing. A skilled DJ knows how to weaponize silence, anticipation, and impact to create moments the crowd will never forget.

Picture this:
- The build-up of a track cuts out, the room goes silent for a beat, and then the bass kicks in at full force.
- You drop a song right as the crowd yells out a key lyric, amplifying their energy tenfold.
- A familiar sample or vocal chop hits unexpectedly, triggering an instant wave of nostalgia and excitement.

These moments don't happen by accident. They come from knowing your music, understanding your crowd, and feeling the pulse of the room in real time.

The Drop as an Energy Shift

The drop is one of the most powerful tools a DJ can use. In EDM, it's a dramatic moment built with tension and release. But in hip-hop, pop, funk, and even wedding sets, the same principle applies. The right drop can cut through the noise and reset the energy of an entire room.

Some tracks are almost guaranteed to bring the room to life when dropped correctly:
- "Feel So Good" – Mase (smooth, feel-good bounce)
- "Crazy in Love" – Beyoncé (instant energy shift)
- "Ain't No Mountain High Enough" – Marvin Gaye & Tammi Terrell (timeless, universal sing-along)

It's not just about the song—it's when and how you deliver it.

Reading the Room and Controlling the Moment

One of the biggest challenges a DJ faces is playing to a mixed crowd. Picture this scenario:
- A group wants to lose themselves in deep house.
- Another crowd lives for '90s hip-hop.
- A handful of guests just want classic rock.
- And then there are the people who only get hyped when they hear a Top 40 hit.

How do you keep everyone engaged?

•Identify the unifying tracks. Every event has those crossover songs that different groups recognize and enjoy. Use these as reset points.

•Understand the flow of energy. Not every moment needs an intense drop—sometimes, a subtle switch is more effective. Learn when to build anticipation and when to go all in.

•Don't force a perfect mix if the moment calls for impact. Some songs demand to be slammed in raw for maximum effect.

In the end, it's about understanding people as much as it's about understanding music.

Master the Drop, Master the Crowd

Technical skills matter. But a DJ who knows how to read energy will always have the upper hand.

A great set isn't just a collection of well-mixed songs —it's a journey. A properly executed drop can be the difference between a forgettable transition and a legendary moment.

Master the drop, and you don't just play music—you dictate the night.

USE THE MICROPHONE.

"Your voice can change the world."
—Nelson Mandela

ACT'N A FOOL

The Power of the Microphone: Commanding the Room as a DJ

Remember when Madonna performed at the 2007 Live Earth concert? She made the bold choice to go mic-free, assuming her presence alone would captivate the audience. It backfired. The crowd struggled to hear her vocals, the energy dropped, and the performance was met with heavy criticism.

As a DJ, your job isn't just to play music—it's to control the vibe, lead the experience, and own the space. If you stay silent behind the decks, blending seamlessly into the background, how will people remember your name? Whether you dream of rocking main stage at a festival or becoming the go-to DJ in your city, staying invisible won't get you there.

You need to be heard.

Why the Microphone is a Game-Changer

A DJ who masters the mic stands out—period. The microphone isn't just for making announcements; it's a bridge between you and the crowd. It's how you connect, guide, and bring your personality to the set.

Think about it. Before booking you, potential clients are asking themselves:

•What does this DJ sound like? Can they energize a room, or do they mumble through announcements?

•Can they manage a crowd? Do they know how to guide guests from one moment to the next without losing momentum?

•Are they professional? Will they say something awkward, offensive, or unplanned?

A DJ who understands the mic's power immediately commands respect—not just from the audience, but from event planners, club owners, and festival bookers. The ability to speak with confidence makes you an asset, not just a music player.

How the Mic Gets You More Gigs

Think about the DJs who get booked the most. They don't just mix well—they engage. They build a connection with the crowd, and the mic is their direct line to making that happen.

Mastering the mic doesn't mean you have to talk nonstop. It means knowing when and how to use it:

✔ Introducing key moments in a set, like transitions or singalong anthems.

✔ Hyping the crowd at peak moments without overdoing it.

✔ Engaging with the audience in a way that feels natural and effortless.

The DJs who master both music and the mic are the ones who get rebooked, recommended, and remembered.

The Mic is More Than a Tool—It's Your Presence

A microphone isn't just an accessory—it's one of the most powerful weapons in your DJ arsenal. It separates the entertainers from the playlist pushers.

So if you're serious about standing out, take control of your voice. Own your presence. Command the room. Let them hear you.

The DJs who stay silent are forgotten. The ones who speak with purpose become legends.

THE BLUEPRINT

Finding Your Voice: Mastering the Mic as a DJ

Using a microphone can feel intimidating. Maybe you don't like the sound of your own voice, or you're afraid of saying the wrong thing. But here's the truth: your voice is an instrument, just like your turntables, mixers, and song selection—and when used correctly, it can be the difference between a forgettable DJ and a legendary one.

When you step behind the decks, your audience has no idea what's coming next. They don't know when the next drop is, when the energy is about to shift, or even who you are. That's where the mic comes in. It's your weapon of engagement, your tool to guide the crowd, and the bridge between you and your audience.

So take a deep breath. Relax. Be natural. Own the moment.

Your Voice is Just as Important as Your Music

By now, you've probably realized that DJing isn't just about mixing records—it's about crafting an experience. If you want to be more than just another DJ, you need to master the art of voice control.

Think about it:
•Weddings: You're introducing the bride and groom. You need poise, confidence, and clarity.
•Bars & Clubs: You're calling last call or setting up a massive drop. Your timing has to be on point.
•Festivals: You're hyping up thousands of people before a beat kicks in. Your energy needs to match the moment.

A DJ who can control the mic with confidence will always be in demand.

How to Improve Your Mic Presence

If talking on the mic doesn't come naturally, don't sweat it. Like everything else in DJing, this is a skill you can sharpen. It just takes the right preparation and mindset.

Here's how to level up your mic game:

✔ Have Go-To Phrases Ready – Build a mental playlist of hype lines that fit different moments. Rehearse them until they flow naturally. Some examples:
"How's everybody feeling tonight?"
"Let's make some noise for the birthday boy/girl!"
"If you're ready for this drop, put your hands up!"

✔ Read the Room & Adapt – Pay attention to what's happening in real-time. If someone's tearing up the dance floor, shout them out. If the energy dips, bring it back up with your words. The best mic work is reactive and in sync with the moment.

✔ Find Your Unique Style – Not every DJ needs to be loud and over-the-top. Some DJs are high-energy hype men, while others have a laid-back, smooth delivery. Experiment and find what works for you.

Command the Room with Confidence

A real DJ doesn't just play music—they control the atmosphere. The mic isn't just a tool; it's your power.

So don't shy away from it. Own it. Use it with intention. Let your voice become part of your set.

Because when you speak with purpose and confidence, people listen. And when people listen? You become unforgettable.

And if ya don't know, now you know, DJ.

Your Voice: The Secret Weapon of a True DJ

Your voice is more than just sound—it's power. It's what transforms a simple DJ set into a fully immersive experience. When wielded correctly, your voice becomes an extension of your artistry, making your presence felt beyond the music.

Because let's be real—anyone can press play. But a real DJ? A real DJ controls the room. They direct the energy, ignite the crowd, and build anticipation before the first beat even drops.

This isn't just about playing music. This is about commanding an atmosphere.

How to Use Your Voice to Elevate Your Set

✔ Build Hype Before the Drop
Ever watched a master DJ before a festival drop? They don't just let the song do the work—they talk to the crowd.
"Y'all ready for this?"
"On the count of three, I want everybody jumping!"
"When this beat drops, I better see hands in the air!"

That split-second anticipation makes the moment explode when the track finally hits.

✔ Engage the Audience & Make Them Feel Part of the Set
A DJ set isn't a performance—it's an experience. The more the crowd feels involved, the more memorable the night becomes.

•Call-and-response: "When I say HEY, you say HO!"

•Crowd check-ins: "Who's celebrating something tonight?"

•Personalized shoutouts: "Big up to my people in the back—y'all still with me?"

When you talk directly to the audience, you break the fourth wall. It's no longer just a party—it's a moment between you and them.

✔ Use Humor & Personality to Stand Out
Cracking jokes. Doing impressions. Throwing in a funny story about how you bombed your first gig. Whatever it is, let your personality show.
A DJ with charisma and wit will always be more memorable than someone who hides behind the decks.

Command the Space Like a Pro

When you blend technical skill with vocal presence, you own the room. It's not just about the music—it's about the total experience.

•Use vocal effects like reverb and delay during transitions for a cinematic touch.

•Control your tone and pacing—speak with confidence, not like you're rushing through an airport announcement.

•Always match the crowd's energy—don't go full hype mode at a black-tie gala, and don't stay quiet at a club.

At the end of the night, the music will end—but if you did your job right, the energy you created will live on.

That's what separates a button-masher from a crowd commander.

Use your voice. Own your presence. And leave them talking about your set long after the lights come on.

THE FLIP SIDE

The Mic Isn't for You? No Problem—Get an MC Who Can Own It

Not every DJ is comfortable on the mic—and that's okay. But here's the thing: somebody has to control the room. If stepping up to the mic isn't your thing, don't just avoid it—delegate it to someone who can do it right.

Enter the MC.

A skilled MC can take your set from dope to legendary. They hype the crowd, guide the energy, and make sure your name is getting the respect it deserves—all while letting you stay locked in on the music.

Why an MC Can Be a Game-Changer

✔ You Focus on the Music, They Handle the Energy
Some DJs prefer to let their music do the talking. That's cool, but in high-energy environments—weddings, nightclubs, festivals—silence between transitions can kill the vibe.
A strong MC keeps the energy alive while you focus on delivering seamless mixes.

✔ They Amplify Your Presence
Your MC isn't just a hype machine—they're a bridge between you and the crowd. They introduce you, remind people who's controlling the decks, and keep your name fresh in everyone's mind.

✔ They Can Read the Room & Guide the Crowd
A skilled MC knows when to bring the energy up, when to cool it down, and how to transition between different vibes without missing a beat. They can direct the crowd without overpowering your set.

How to Find the Right MC

If you're bringing someone on board, make sure they fit the vibe you're curating. Your MC should:

•Have stage presence – A monotone MC kills momentum. Find someone who can command attention without forcing it.

•Have a clean, clear voice – If the crowd can't understand what they're saying, it's just noise.

•Understand the event – A club MC and a wedding MC are two different beasts. Choose accordingly.

The DJ & MC Dynamic: A Winning Formula

Some of the most iconic DJ duos in history have thrived on this balance:

•DJ Jazzy Jeff & The Fresh Prince – The DJ provided the beats, the MC kept the energy electric.

•Grandmaster Flash & The Furious Five – One of hip-hop's pioneering combinations of DJ & MC synergy.

Having the right MC isn't just a workaround for avoiding the mic—it's a power move. It allows you to focus entirely on crafting a flawless musical journey while your MC enhances the experience, ensuring the audience stays engaged, hyped, and connected.

At the end of the day, DJing isn't just about spinning tracks. It's about owning the room—and if you're not the one on the mic, make sure someone's got it covered.

FAMILIARIZE YOURSELF WITH ALL GENRES OF MUSIC.

"The man who reads nothing at all is better educated than the man who reads nothing but newspapers."
—Thomas Jefferson

ACT'N A FOOL

Adapt or Be Left Behind: The Power of Versatility in DJing

I once invited a DJ friend to join me for a gig. The bag was secured, the crowd was ready, and the only thing standing in the way was one simple request: the client wanted a mix of pop, '80s, and vintage rock—not just hip-hop and R&B.

My friend declined.

Instead of researching the genres, asking for advice, or treating it as a chance to level up, she passed on the opportunity. The result? She missed out on the money, the connections, and the experience—all because she wasn't willing to step outside of her comfort zone.

That moment was a wake-up call. As a DJ, adaptability is your lifeline.

Your Personal Taste vs. Your Audience's Needs

Being a DJ isn't about flexing your personal playlist —it's about reading the room and delivering what the crowd needs. You might love underground house, but if you're at a wedding, you better have Earth, Wind & Fire in your crate. You might swear by hip-hop, but if a corporate event wants 80s pop classics, that's what you're playing. You might be all about techno, but if a

Latin crowd wants salsa and reggaeton, you'd better pivot.

The best DJs don't just mix songs—they understand culture, nostalgia, and audience psychology. Music is memory, and the right song at the right time creates moments people will never forget.

Expanding Your Repertoire = Expanding Your Career

The more genres you master, the more gigs you can book. A DJ who can seamlessly transition from hip-hop to classic rock to house is infinitely more valuable than one who only sticks to one lane. Versatility doesn't just get you more work—it makes you a better artist.

Here's how you start expanding:
- Study New Genres: Spend time exploring playlists outside of your usual taste. Learn song structures and energy patterns.
- Ask Other DJs for Advice: If you don't know disco, find a DJ who does. If you need rock knowledge, ask a specialist.
- Use Streaming Services: Services like Spotify, Apple Music, and YouTube have curated playlists for nearly every genre.
- Test Different Styles: Start small—blend a new genre into your usual set and see how the crowd reacts.

Being a DJ Means Always Being a Student

No matter how long you've been in the game, you'll always have something to learn. Every gig is a lesson in human psychology, musical evolution, and crowd control. Some crowds will challenge you. Some sets will test your skills. But the DJs who embrace those moments instead of avoiding them? They're the ones who last.

It's simple: adapt or be left behind. If you're serious about building a lasting career, don't just play what you like—become the DJ that can play anything, anytime, for anyone. That's how you get booked. That's how you get respect. That's how you win.

THE BLUEPRINT

Building a Timeless, Crowd-Captivating Music Library

If you want to stand out as a DJ, your music library needs to be unmatched. A killer set isn't just about playing hit songs—it's about knowing what to play, when to play it, and how to blend it into something unforgettable.

Versatility is Your Secret Weapon

Your ability to seamlessly navigate across genres, eras, and vibes is what sets you apart from the pack. A wedding crowd expects a different energy than a nightclub. A festival demands a different pace than a corporate event. A DJ who only plays one style limits their bookings and their growth. A DJ who can move from hip-hop to house to funk to pop? That's a crowd controller.

It's not just about what you like—it's about what the audience responds to. The more you understand different musical styles, the more you can create unforgettable moments that keep people talking long after the party ends.

Understanding Track Structure = Better Mixing

Every DJ should know their music inside and out. It's not just about having hot songs in your library—it's about knowing the best moments within those songs.

Take "Ride Wit Me" by Nelly as an example. Instead of playing the entire track, break it down:
- Start with the chorus – Instant energy boost.
- Hit them with the iconic verse – That "I know something you don't know" line gets the crowd rapping along.
- Loop back into the chorus – Keep them locked in and exit strong before the song overstays its welcome.

This technique applies to any genre. Whether you're playing 90s hip-hop, house music, or reggaeton, knowing the strongest moments of a track allows you to control energy levels and keep your set moving without dead zones.

Your Digital Crate: Where to Find New Music

A modern DJ has access to more music than ever before, and if you're not constantly expanding your library, you're falling behind.

- Streaming Services – Apple Music, Spotify, and Tidal offer deep catalogs that help you research, discover, and organize playlists before purchasing tracks.
- DJ Pools – Platforms like BPM Supreme, DJ City, and Digital DJ Pool give you remixes, edits, and exclusive versions that keep your sets sounding fresh.
- YouTube, SoundCloud, & Mixcloud – These platforms expose you to underground talent, international sounds, and unique remixes you won't find anywhere else.
- Shazam & Music Blogs – Never miss a dope track. Whether you're at a bar or listening to a set, Shazam will identify tracks instantly, and music blogs will keep you ahead of trends.

The Art of Curating a Library That Works for Every Crowd

Building an extensive library isn't about hoarding songs—it's about curating a collection of music that works for every type of crowd you'll encounter.

- Essential Classics – Songs that always get a reaction (Michael Jackson, Beyoncé, Tupac, Biggie, Prince, Madonna).
- Current Chart-Toppers – Stay updated with what's trending so your sets feel fresh.

- Deep Cuts & Remixes – The hidden gems that set you apart from every other DJ playing basic Top 40 hits.

- Regional Hits – If you're playing for a Latin crowd, you better know your reggaeton and salsa. In New Orleans? Bounce music is key. Know your crowd's culture and meet them where they are.

Stay Hungry, Stay Ahead

A DJ's job isn't just playing music—it's knowing how to curate, blend, and reinvent it in a way that keeps crowds locked in. Constantly discovering new artists, understanding track structure, and refining your transitions will separate you from the amateurs.

Music is constantly evolving. The question is: Are you evolving with it?

THE FLIP SIDE

Mastering Your Craft & Expanding Your Sound

Versatility is your superpower as a DJ—but true mastery lies in knowing your genre inside and out. This is where the legends separate themselves from the amateurs. Study the history of your chosen style. Learn its roots, cultural influence, and the innovators who shaped its evolution. Know it so well that when someone plays a track, you can instantly recognize the production techniques, the era it came from, and how it fits into a larger musical movement.

But don't box yourself in. The best DJs are the ones who can take their foundation and build upon it with new sounds. Expand your knowledge by exploring adjacent subgenres, drawing inspiration from different styles, and incorporating unexpected elements into your sets. Every genre has a story, and the more you understand, the more creative you can be behind the decks.

Digging Deeper: The Tools of the Trade

With today's technology, you have no excuse to stay in a musical bubble. Use tools like Shazam to track down obscure records and hidden gems. Follow DJ record pools and specialty playlists to stay ahead of trends. Apps like Mixed In Key can help you understand the harmonic structure of your favorite songs, so your transitions feel smoother and more intentional. Serato also has a plugin.

Networking is just as critical as digging for tracks. Build strong relationships with other DJs, producers, and promoters. Get featured in their sets. Exchange song recommendations. The more you collaborate, the faster you'll grow. You never know who might put you on to your next big opportunity.

And here's a little-known secret: Take dance lessons. Understanding how different genres move the human body will transform the way you mix. If you see how a salsa rhythm translates to movement, you'll know exactly when to cut or extend a track. If you recognize how hip-hop dancers react to beat switches, you'll structure your transitions with precision. Your job isn't just to play music—it's to control the energy of the room.

The Science of Crowd Control

Every gig is a chance to study people as much as music. When you're at a party or club, observe.

Which songs make people lose their minds?

What BPMs tend to keep them moving versus making them tired?

Do they react better to sing-along anthems or deep cuts?

These small details are gold. The more you analyze crowd behavior, the more intuitive your set-building becomes.

As Victor Hugo once said, "Music expresses that which cannot be said and on which it is impossible to be silent." Your job as a DJ is to translate that energy into an experience. The better you understand your music, your crowd, and your craft, the more unforgettable your performances will be.

So study. Expand. Connect. And most of all—experiment.

PAY ATTENTION TO THE PARTY.

"The secret of health for both mind and body is not to mourn for the past, nor to worry about the future, but to live in the present moment wisely and earnestly."
—Buddha

ACT'N A FOOL

DJing isn't just about dropping fire mixes—it's about reading the room and connecting with the people in it. You could have the cleanest transitions and the dopest track selection, but if you're locked into your laptop the whole time, you might as well be a playlist on shuffle. A great DJ doesn't just play music; they command the energy of the room.

Your set should paint a picture that moves people, and the only way to do that is to watch, listen, and respond to the crowd.

The Moment That Changed Everything

Early in my career, I learned this lesson the hard way. I was obsessed with perfection—plotting every transition down to the second, making sure every mix was surgically tight. When I DJed my first wedding (shoutout to James and Rachel Mulkey!), I was so focused on sticking to my plan that I forgot to actually watch the crowd.

The set was flawless, but the energy? Flat. And that's my bad, Mulkey's.

I was mixing for myself, not the people in front of me. I missed key moments where I could've hyped up the room, taken requests, or simply made eye contact to gauge reactions. The night was technically solid—but emotionally, it fell short.

Crowd Connection: The Real Secret to a Legendary Set

The DJs who last in this game are the ones who know how to control a crowd. That doesn't just mean playing bangers—it means understanding when to drop them, when to switch the vibe, and how to make people feel seen and heard.

Here's how you make sure you're always locked in with your audience:

1. Establish Eye Contact

Look up. Engage. Feel the crowd. A single head nod, a smile, or a knowing glance can make people feel like they're a part of something bigger.

2. Feel the Vibe & Adjust

You're not just pressing play—you're orchestrating the experience. If people are zoning out, it's time to switch gears. Maybe they need something with more bass, or maybe they need a throwback they can scream at the top of their lungs. Stay flexible.

3. Show Enthusiasm

Energy is contagious. If you're vibing behind the decks, the crowd will mirror that energy. If you look stiff or uninterested, they'll feel it. Even if you're nervous, own the moment.

4. Balance Between Technicality & Engagement

Yes, your mix needs to be tight. Yes, your transitions should be clean. But DJing isn't just about execution—it's about presence. Strike a balance between staying focused on your craft and making sure the people in front of you are having the time of their lives.

The Difference Between Good DJs & Great DJs

Good DJs play music.
Great DJs play the crowd.

When you stop thinking of your set as a pre-planned playlist and start treating it like a conversation, that's when you level up. Pay attention, be in the moment, and let your presence electrify the room.

As Stevie Wonder said:

"Music, if rightly understood, is a spiritual experience."

That spirit isn't just in the songs—it's in the connection between you and your audience. Make it count.

THE BLUEPRINT

Command the Room Like a Pro

As the DJ, you are the pulse of the party—the unseen force that controls the energy of the room. You don't just play music; you curate an experience. Every transition, every drop, every pause in the music is an opportunity to heighten anticipation, shift the mood, and take your crowd on a journey. Neither does the impact of a DJ who knows how to read a crowd and deliver unforgettable moments.

The Science of Reading the Room

Think of yourself as a social scientist behind the decks:

1. Observe the Crowd
   - What's the age range? A younger crowd might want modern hits, while an older audience may lean toward throwbacks.
   - What's the event type? A corporate gathering is different from a festival set or a wedding after-party.
   - What's their energy level? Are they lively and engaged, or is the dance floor looking thin?

2. Tailor Your Set in Real-Time
   - If the dance floor is packed, keep the energy high and maintain momentum.
   - If people are standing around, mix in familiar tracks to hook them in.

- If the crowd is a mixed bag, blend genres—find common ground with universally loved anthems.

Engagement: Your Secret Weapon

Your energy is contagious. If you're hyped, they're hyped. If you look like you're just going through the motions, they'll feel it.

How to Command the Room Like a Pro

- Use the Mic With Purpose – Hype up the crowd at key moments. Call and response works wonders.
- Make Eye Contact – Let the crowd know you see them, feel their energy, and are there to elevate their night.
- Listen & Adapt – No matter if guests are singing/ rapping to the lyrics or if the crowd is mingling with each other, they're giving you direct feedback. Use it.

Before the Gig: Do Your Homework

Being a great DJ starts before you press play.

1. Know the Event
- What's the crowd size? A packed nightclub requires different energy than an intimate lounge set.
- Is there a theme? If it's an '80s party, have deep cuts ready—don't just play the obvious hits.
- Who's the client? A corporate booking might want clean edits, while a late-night crowd might prefer raw, unfiltered energy.

2. Connect with the Key Players

Your job isn't just to rock the party—it's to make everyone involved in the event look good. Build relationships with:
- Event planners – They might refer you for future gigs.
- Bartenders – They know the crowd and can give insight on the vibe.
- Venue staff – They control the lights, sound, and layout—get on their good side.

Signature Moments: Stand Out From the Rest

Anyone can play music, but only a few DJs create moments that stick with people.
- Take advantage of unique opportunities – If the bar announces free shots at midnight, time your music to hype up that moment.
- Know when to drop a classic anthem – That one track that unites the room and gets people screaming the lyrics? Be ready for it.
- Create an unforgettable finale – A well-crafted closing song leaves people on a high note and makes them remember YOU.

Pro Tips for Owning the Night

• Listen to the room – The best DJs are always observing, adjusting, and responding.
• Monitor the dance floor – Are people engaged or starting to wander off? Adapt accordingly.

• Respect requests—but control the flow – You don't have to play everything, but if a song fits, use it to your advantage.

• Be approachable – A DJ who interacts with the crowd builds stronger connections and leaves a lasting impression.

Final Thoughts: The DJ is the Energy Architect

Every beat, every transition, every second behind the decks is an opportunity to craft a moment people will never forget.

Your mission?
- Set the tone.
- Keep the energy flowing.
- Make the crowd feel like they're part of something special.

Because as Bono once said:

"Music can change the world because it can change people."

And as a DJ, that's the power you hold.

Remember, DJ: You are in control.

The Art of Networking Without Selling

A packed dance floor is great, but a loyal fanbase is priceless. Pay close attention to the people who truly vibe with your sound—the ones singing along, hyping you up, and locking in with your set. These are your ambassadors. They'll be the ones spreading your name, tagging you on social media, and bringing friends to your gigs.

But don't just hope they remember you. Make the connection stick.

When you're out there, introduce yourself with confidence and authenticity. Say their name back to them in conversation—it's a small move that makes a big impact. It shows respect, attention, and makes you instantly more memorable. People don't just remember great music; they remember how you made them feel.

How to Turn Every Interaction Into a Business Opportunity

1. Engage With Purpose—Beyond Small Talk

Anyone can ask, "Hey, did you have fun tonight?" but a real pro goes deeper. Strike up conversations that actually mean something.
- Ask about their upcoming events. Who knows? They might need a DJ.
- Find out what kind of vibe they love. Their answer can help you refine your sound or introduce them to something new.

- Listen for opportunities. People will casually mention birthdays, weddings, or corporate events— moments where they need music. That's your cue.

The goal isn't to sell—it's to build trust. When people feel like you actually care, they'll want to book you.

2. Create Branding That Speaks for You

Your presence should be felt even after the music stops.
- Business Cards That Stand Out: Forget the generic black-and-white cards everyone tosses in a drawer. Make yours look like a mixtape—your name on the front, contact details styled as a tracklist on the back. It's a conversation starter before they even hear your set.
- Wear Your Brand: Got a logo? A signature look? Incorporate it into your gear. Subtle details—a branded snapback, custom stickers on your laptop—keep you recognizable without looking like a walking ad.
- QR Codes Are Your Friend: Slap a QR code on your business card or laptop that links to your latest mix, booking page, or social media. Make it effortless for people to stay connected.

3. Build a Network That Elevates Your Game

No DJ succeeds alone.
- Connect with photographers and videographers at events. High-quality visuals are gold for your brand. If you're just starting out, find creatives who are also building their portfolios—trade services and grow together.

- Work with event planners, venue managers, and promoters. When they need a reliable DJ, you want to be the first name they think of.
- Support other DJs. Too many DJs see each other as competition. The smart ones see an opportunity—guest sets, collabs, and referrals lead to more gigs.

4. Give Before You Ask

Want to leave a lasting impression? Help before you hustle.

Nobody likes someone who only shows up when they need something. Instead, be the person who adds value first.
- Share a helpful tip with another DJ.
- Recommend a venue to an event planner.
- Give genuine compliments and shoutouts to performers you respect.

People remember generosity. When the time comes for them to refer a DJ, your name will be the first one they mention.

Every gig, every event, every conversation is a chance to solidify your reputation—not just as a DJ, but as someone who understands and cares about their audience.

A great set gets people moving.
A great connection keeps them coming back.

So keep it real. Be helpful. Let your passion do the talking.

THE FLIP SIDE

One of the most powerful roles of a DJ is connection. Without it, you're just spinning tracks in an empty room. It's like throwing a party without music—there's no energy, no synergy, no magic. The crowd isn't just a group of people; they're an extension of your set, and every drop, blend, and transition is an invitation to be part of something bigger than just sound.

But here's the catch—not every gig is worth your time.

Yes, every event is an opportunity to earn, expand your network, and solidify your name, but not every booking aligns with your vision, values, or brand. The best DJs don't just play music—they curate experiences that reflect who they are. That means knowing when to say yes and, just as importantly, knowing when to say no.

Protecting Your Brand: The Yelp Lesson

Let me put it like this—I once had a 13-year-old reach out to me via Yelp, asking to book me for her birthday party. Her mom had given her permission to contact me directly, but I wasn't comfortable handling business with a minor online. So I did what any professional should do

—I politely asked her to connect me with her parents instead.

Unfortunately, she didn't take it well. She felt like I was doubting her maturity, and before I knew it, she and her mom hit me with a one-star review, calling me disrespectful.

Now, let's be real—nobody likes getting bad reviews. But instead of seeing it as a hit to my reputation, I saw it for what it really was—a reflection of my principles.

When potential clients read that review, I hope they see more than just a rating. I hope they see a DJ who takes his work seriously, respects boundaries, and refuses to cut corners—because those qualities matter. In fact, they matter more than any single booking.

Your Reputation Is Your Currency

Your values are your backbone. Your reputation is your currency. As the legendary Nina Simone once said, "You've got to learn to leave the table when love's no longer being served." In other words, stand firm in your principles—even when it costs you a booking, a review, or an opportunity.

The best DJs don't just play music—they build trust. They create a brand that speaks for itself. They earn respect, not by chasing every dollar, but by staying authentic, delivering excellence, and never compromising their standards. So next time you face a questionable gig or a situation that doesn't sit right, ask yourself:

Is this an opportunity—or a compromise?

Does this align with my values—or does it undercut them?

Will this gig elevate my reputation—or put it at risk?

The DJs who last—the ones who get booked again and again—aren't the ones who say yes to everything. They're the ones who say yes to the right things.

Stay true. Stay sharp. And let your reputation be louder than any review.

CLEAN YOURSELF UP.

"Dress shabbily and they remember the dress; dress impeccably and they remember the woman."
—Coco Chanel

ACT'N A FOOL

The Look, The Feel, The Performance—It All Matters

I had a gig in New York City once, and in the chaos of prepping for the night, I skipped a crucial detail—a haircut. I didn't think much of it until I caught my reflection before the show. I looked like Will Smith in Emancipation.

Not exactly the energy I wanted to walk in with.

From that moment on, I felt off. My confidence took a hit, and as I made my way to the venue, that insecurity crept into my head. Even though I delivered a killer performance, those discouraging thoughts never let up. No one in the crowd knew what was going on in my mind—but I did. And that's the thing: how you feel about yourself directly affects how you command a room.

Energy Over Appearance—But Both Matter

Here's the real lesson: Your presence is your power.

Yes, talent speaks louder than anything, but how you present yourself sets the tone before you even touch the decks. When you feel good, you perform better. But even on days when you don't feel your best, your ability to own the room, control the energy, and bring undeniable passion is what leaves a lasting impression.

As Prince once said, "Despite everything, no one can dictate who you are to other people."

That means even when you're not feeling like your sharpest self, you still have the power to own the moment —but it starts with mindset.

Command Every Room, Every Time

After that night, I made it a priority to leave time for the small details that keep me feeling confident—because when you're at your best, you perform at your peak.

But the biggest lesson? Even when things aren't perfect, your execution is what defines you.

So next time you're doubting yourself—whether it's your look, your mood, or something else that's messing with your head—channel that energy into your set. Turn every insecurity into fuel.

Let every drop remind you who you are.
Let every transition sharpen your focus.
Let every beat be a statement that nothing—not even a bad hair day—can throw you off your game.

Because when you step behind those decks, it's all about what you bring to the music, the moment, and the people in front of you. Everything else? Secondary.

THE BLUEPRINT

Presentation is Part of the Brand

Taking care of your hygiene might seem like common sense, but you'd be shocked at how many DJs overlook this fundamental part of their personal brand. Whether you're headlining a festival, rocking a club, or setting the mood at a private event, your look is a reflection of your professionalism.

First impressions matter. You could have the best set of the night, but if you roll up looking sloppy, it sends the wrong message before you even touch the decks.

For DJs, personal grooming isn't just about looking presentable—it's part of your brand identity. Clients and fans aren't just tuning in for the music; they're drawn to the energy you project. When you present yourself as sharp, put-together, and polished, you instantly command respect.

Think about it—when you see a DJ that looks the part, you assume they know what they're doing. When you see one who looks like they just rolled out of bed? Different story.

Here's how to keep yourself looking fresh, without overcomplicating the process.

Hair Care: Stay Sharp

If you rock short hair, schedule a fresh cut every week or two. If you're growing it out, keep it trimmed and styled. Hair is a big part of your presence, and whether it's a sharp fade, twists, or slicked-back locks, make sure it's intentional.

Pro Tip: If you want a signature look, experiment with styles that complement your personality and brand. Just make sure it doesn't look unintentional or unkempt.

Wardrobe Essentials: Fit the Scene, But Stay You

Your outfit doesn't need to be expensive—it just needs to be clean, intentional, and fit the vibe of your event.
- Private & Corporate Gigs: Keep it polished. A tailored blazer, dress shirt, and fitted slacks go a long way. You don't need to wear a suit, but looking refined will get you booked again.
- Club & Festival Gigs: This is where you can flex your personal style—graphic tees, bold colors, or a statement jacket all work. Just make sure it fits well and looks fresh.
- Casual & Day Events: Even if the event is laid-back, you should never look like you just woke up. Crisp jeans, clean sneakers, and a well-fitted tee will keep you looking effortlessly cool.

Remember: Your wardrobe should complement your music and brand, not work against it.

On-the-Go Grooming Kit: Stay Fresh, Always

DJs are always moving—flights, long nights, and back-to-back gigs can make it hard to stay fresh. But that's why you need your on-the-go grooming kit. Keep a small toiletry bag with:

- Gum & Mints (Nobody wants to talk to a DJ with Shrek breath.)
- Face Wipes & Lotion (Quick refresh between gigs.)
- Toothbrush & Travel Mouthwash (For when you don't have time to hit the hotel.)
- Deodorant or Cologne/Perfume (Because smelling good is non-negotiable.)
- Lip Balm & Eye Drops (Late nights can dry you out—stay looking alive.)

Why It Matters

Hygiene and presentation are about more than just appearances. It's about confidence. When you feel fresh, you perform better, interact with more ease, and exude professionalism.

So before you walk into your next gig, take a minute to check yourself. Are you presenting the image of a DJ who takes their craft seriously? If not, step it up—because whether you like it or not, the way you show up is part of the gig.

And if you ever feel like skipping that haircut or rolling in looking reckless, remember this: If you don't take yourself seriously, why should anyone else?

THE FLIP SIDE

Know When to Get Dirty

Some gigs demand suit-and-tie professionalism. Others? You're in the trenches, getting wild with the crowd. Foam parties, beach raves, poolside sets, muddy festivals—these aren't the places to worry about keeping your sneakers pristine.

If you're playing a gig where getting messy is part of the experience, lean into it. Rock your older kicks, throw on a pair of shorts, maybe even a headband or some face paint to match the vibe. You don't show up to a jungle rave in dress shoes, and you don't DJ a Spartan race in a tux.

But let's talk about the other side of the coin.

When you're spinning from your bedroom for an online audience, you might think, "No one can smell me, so why bother cleaning up?" But here's the thing—your energy translates, even through the screen. Feeling fresh boosts confidence, and confidence enhances performance.

So yeah, match the energy of the event, but don't let yourself slide into sloppiness. Whether you're in a club, on a livestream, or deep in the mud at a festival, you are still a professional.

Know the Difference: When to Dress Up & When to Get Down

The 'Cleaned Up' Look—For Professional Gigs
•Weddings, Corporate Events, Upscale Clubs → A well-fitted blazer, clean sneakers or dress shoes, and a fresh lineup or styled hair. You're being paid to bring the vibe, but also to look like someone worth paying.

The 'Controlled Chaos' Look—For High-Energy Party Gigs
•Festivals, Foam Parties, Theme Events → It's about intentional casual. Wear something that fits the event without looking like you just rolled out of bed.

The 'Sweat-Soaked Madness' Look—For the Wild Ones
•Spartan Races, Beach Gigs, Underground Raves → No one expects you to be pristine, but they do expect you to own your look. Confidence is everything.

Bottom Line: Take Yourself Seriously, Even When the Gig is Messy

Whether you're dressed to impress or embracing the grime, it all comes back to one thing—presence. How you present yourself affects how people perceive you, how they remember you, and ultimately, how often they book you.

So go ahead, get wild when the gig calls for it. Just make sure, underneath the sweat and confetti, your professionalism stays spotless.

BE AN ACTIVE LISTENER.

"We have two ears and one mouth so that we can listen twice as much as we speak."

—Epictetus

ACT'N A FOOL

Shit Happens.

Being a great DJ isn't just about blending tracks—it's about reading the room, planning for the unexpected, and handling chaos like a pro. Any DJ can hit play, but the real ones know how to adapt, anticipate, and execute flawlessly.

Expect the Unexpected (Because It's Coming)

The unexpected isn't a maybe—it's a guarantee. Gear will fail, event organizers will forget to tell you crucial details, and venues will promise equipment that turns out to be absolute garbage. You either plan for these moments, or you get blindsided.

Here's How You Stay Ahead of the Bullshit:

Ask the Right Questions Before Every Gig
- What sound system is available? Get photos. Get specs.
- Where will you be set up? Is there power nearby?
- Who's running the event? Are they actually competent, or just hyped-up amateurs?
- What's the crowd expecting? High-energy bangers? Smooth dinner vibes? A mix?

Never assume anything. Get details in writing, confirm twice, and prepare for the worst.

Take Control of Your Setup

Relying on someone else's gear? Treat it as a backup, not your primary.
- Always bring extra cables, adapters, and a backup USB or laptop.
- Carry your own mic. Never assume the venue has a working one.
- If using house speakers, test them early. If they suck, have a Plan B.

A pro DJ takes ownership of their performance. If the sound is trash, it's your reputation on the line—not the venue's.

Stay Hyper-Aware at the Event
- Read the room like a mind-reader. Who's vibing? Who's disengaged? Adjust accordingly.
- Pay attention to the venue's acoustics. Some spaces drown out bass, others amplify it too much. Adapt your EQ in real-time.
- Watch the bartenders and servers. If drinks are flowing and energy is rising, it's time to build up the set.

Real-World Example: The Wedding Speaker Disaster That Wasn't

I once got booked for a wedding where the venue told me, "Don't worry, we have speakers for you." Now, I've been in this game long enough to know that means, "We have random speakers lying around that may or may not actually work."

So I asked for photos and details. They never sent them.

Rather than rolling the dice, I brought my own setup. And guess what? Their so-called "PA system" was actually just a pair of small home theater speakers. Had I trusted them, the couple's big day would have been a disaster, with guests struggling to hear the music. Instead, because I was prepared, the night went off flawlessly, and I walked away with new referrals and a bigger reputation.

The Bottom Line: Take Charge or Take the L

If you don't actively listen, plan ahead, and control your setup, you're setting yourself up for failure. The best DJs don't just play music—they run the show.

So before every gig, get your answers, double-check your setup, and stay locked in from the first beat to the last. That's how you go from just another DJ to an untouchable pro.

THE BLUEPRINT

The Best DJs Read the Room

Being a DJ isn't just about dropping fire tracks—it's about tuning into the energy of the crowd and using that knowledge to elevate the experience. Every move you make behind the decks should be informed by what's happening on the dance floor, at the bar, and even in the quiet corners of the venue.

You're not just playing music—you're controlling the entire vibe of the night.

The Art of Reading the Room

A real DJ watches, listens, and adapts. The way people dance, what they're talking about, even what they're drinking—it all tells a story.

Here's how to decode the crowd and keep the party alive:

✅ Watch the Body Language
   •   Are people locked in, vibing with your set?
   •   Are they nodding their heads but hesitant to hit the floor?
   •   Are they standing around with drinks, waiting for the right song to drop?

Your job is to adjust on the fly. If the energy is high, keep feeding it. If they're waiting for a reason to dance, give them one—hit them with a familiar hook or a remix that flips the mood instantly.

✅ Listen to the Room

•What's the chatter like? If people are engaged in deep convos, don't force bangers too early. Build up gradually.

•If the bartenders are slammed, that means people are getting loose. Time to bring out those undeniable dancefloor anthems.

•If servers are handing out cake at a wedding, that's a natural transition for a mood shift—maybe a slow jam or a classic sing-along before ramping up the energy again.

Blend Music with the Crowd's Pulse

If a group of bachelorettes are wilding out, lean into their vibe. Toss in a nostalgic anthem or a song they have to scream along to. If the older crowd is feeling left out, throw in a timeless groove to bridge the gap. If the room is split between different musical tastes, find a track that unites them all.

The Power of Asking the Right Questions

Active listening starts before you even step behind the decks.

Too many DJs assume things will be handled—the venue will have the right setup, the event planner will be on top of the timeline, the crowd will just magically respond. That's a rookie mistake.

Instead, ask smart questions ahead of time:

"Do you guys have extension cords?"

"What's the power situation like? How many outlets are near the DJ booth?"

"What's the vibe of the event?"

"What kind of crowd are you expecting? What's the age range, and are there any must-play or must-avoid tracks?"

If the answers sound vague or unsure, take control and prepare for worst-case scenarios. Bring your own extension cords, extra cables, and backups for everything. If the event planner doesn't have a timeline, make your own.

A DJ who plans ahead and listens closely is untouchable.

Command the Room Like an MC

Listening isn't just about the music—it's about being the trusted voice of the event.

You're not just the DJ. You're the master of ceremonies. That means:

•Engaging with party planners, bartenders, and servers. These people hold key insights on how the night is flowing.

•Helping out when needed. If you see the couple at a wedding stressing over last-minute details, offer to coordinate an announcement or adjust your set to ease the pressure.

•Owning the mic when necessary. Don't just assume the music will do all the work. A well-placed

"Alright, let's get this party started!" can set the tone for the entire night.

The DJs Who Listen Win—Every Time

Great DJs don't just play music. They listen. They adjust. They lead.

If you want to be the DJ everyone remembers, you need to:
- Stay locked into the energy of the room.
- Anticipate what the crowd needs before they even realize it.
- Ask the right questions and come over-prepared.
 Command the event like a true professional.

Because at the end of the night, the best DJs aren't just heard. They're felt.

THE FLIP SIDE

When I say "listen," I don't mean just nodding along like a damn robot while a client rambles on about their favorite songs. I mean engaged, strategic listening—the kind that elevates you from just another DJ to an in-demand professional.

Why Listening is Your Competitive Edge

Your job isn't just to hit play. It's to understand the crowd, predict the energy, and curate an experience. That starts long before you even plug in your gear.

When a client requests music, don't just hear them—analyze what they're saying. Are they asking for a vibe that fits the event, or are they just listing their personal favorites? There's a difference.

For example, if a corporate client tells you they want "hip-hop," what do they actually mean? Are they thinking classic Nas and Biggie, or do they want Travis Scott and Cardi B? Your job is to break it down.

If a bride and groom request explicit trap bangers at their wedding but their guest list includes grandparents and kids, you owe it to them to gently guide them toward clean edits or a better mix that keeps everyone happy.

Set the Tone Before the Event Even Starts

Don't wait until the gig starts to have tough conversations. Manage expectations early. Ask the right questions:

"What's the age range of your guests?"

"Is there a specific moment where you want high-energy tracks?"

"Are there any must-play or do-not-play songs?"

Offer expert guidance:

"I can definitely play your favorite tracks, but let's consider clean versions so the whole crowd stays engaged."

"If we save this track for later in the night, it'll hit harder when people are more warmed up."

Know when to walk away:

If a club promoter, event manager, or client tries to undercut your expertise or disrespect your role, don't be afraid to decline the gig. No paycheck is worth sacrificing your reputation or dealing with someone who doesn't respect what you bring to the table.

Listening is More Than Just Sound—It's Strategy

Active listening isn't about mindless agreement—it's about absorbing, processing, and making smart, professional decisions. It's what separates the amateurs from the pros.

Listen beyond words—watch for body language, tone, and reactions.

Pay attention to how people respond on the dance floor. Every shift in energy tells you something.

Know your boundaries and set expectations. Never let anyone dictate your performance if it compromises your standards.

Keep your ears open, your instincts sharp, and your professionalism intact. The DJs who truly listen are the ones who get booked again and again.

SOCIAL MEDIA IS A DOUBLE EDGED SWORD. KNOW THE DIFFERENCE.

"Humbleness is not thinking less of yourself, it's thinking of yourself less."
—C.S. Lewis

ACT'N A FOOL

I knew a DJ who lived and breathed music. Every set he played was pure fire—his energy, his passion, the way he crafted sound to move people was untouchable. And he knew how to share that gift. His social media wasn't just a highlight reel; it was a living, breathing extension of his artistry. Every post, every video, every mix pulled people in and kept them locked.

Then one day, he blew up. One viral clip, and overnight, his name was everywhere. But something changed.

Instead of keeping it about the music, he made it all about himself. His content stopped being about the crowd, the art, the experience—it turned into a never-ending broadcast of self-promotion. It wasn't about making people feel something anymore; it was about flexing. And just like that, the same audience that built him up began to tune out.

Social Media Can Build or Break You

For DJs, social media is a tool, not a throne. It's a way to connect, inspire, and elevate your craft—but when used wrong, it can also be your downfall.

Too many DJs fall into the trap of thinking their online presence is just about showing off. The flashy gear, the VIP parties, the name-dropping—it's all noise unless it serves a purpose. People don't connect with arrogance—they connect with authenticity.

The DJs who win the social media game are the ones who give their audience something real. They don't just post for validation—they post for impact.

How to Win the Social Game Without Losing Yourself

Social media isn't your personal shrine—it's a platform to bring value. Instead of "Look at me!", think "How can I entertain, educate, or inspire?" Give your audience something they can use, feel, or vibe with.

Engagement is everything. It's not about stacking followers; it's about building relationships. Reply to comments. Ask questions. Share others' wins. Treat your followers like a community, not a fanbase. Recognize the people who support you—shout them out, interact, and keep it real.

There's nothing wrong with flexing, but balance it with substance. Yes, showcase your highlights, but don't just post "Big moves only!" content. Show the grind, the process, the journey. People relate to struggle and growth, not just success. The raw, unpolished moments build more connection than perfectly curated ones.

Your content should speak to the culture. Think about commercials. The best ones don't just sell a product—they sell a feeling. Approach your content the same way. Instead of posting, "Here's my new mix," create something that makes people feel like they need to hear it. Let them know this mix will change the way they feel about 90s hip-hop. Make them curious, make them invested.

Above all, stay humble. Social media will gas you up, but don't believe your own hype too much. The second you start thinking you're bigger than the music, the people, or the culture—you've already lost.

Final Word: Play the Long Game

Social media isn't a sprint—it's a marathon. If you build your presence on giving people something meaningful, you'll create a real, loyal following that sticks with you for the long haul.

Stay humble, intentional, and authentic, and your name won't just be trending—you'll be respected.

THE BLUEPRINT

Social Media is Your Stage—But Don't Be the Clown

Almost everybody is locked into social media these days—millions of people glued to their screens, scrolling, sharing, engaging. So why wouldn't you want to put yourself in front of them? But here's the twist—you don't want to be just another DJ screaming for attention. You want to be the one people talk about without you having to say a word.

Let the Crowd Hype You

I'll never forget when someone caught a clip of me DJing at a pool party and said, "He's actually DJing! Wow." That video blew up, and suddenly, I had all these new eyes on me—not because I was hyping myself up, but because someone else did it for me. That unsolicited reaction hit harder than any self-promotion ever could. It was raw, real, and believable. That's the kind of energy you want behind your name.

If you constantly scream, "Look at me! I'm the best DJ ever!" people will tune you out. But if someone else says, "Yo, this DJ is insane—you gotta check him out," now you've got their attention. Social proof is everything. People believe other people more than they believe marketing. So instead of just posting clips of yourself with some overused caption, make sure your content includes real reactions, audience energy, and the moments that make people feel something.

Engage, Don't Just Post

Social media is the game, and conversation is the currency. Your goal isn't just to post content—it's to spark reactions, make people engage, and trigger that share button. You want people tagging their friends, debating in the comments, and hyping you up before you even step into the booth. And to do that, you have to be remarkable.

Here's the mistake too many DJs make: they treat social media like a billboard instead of a conversation. They post their set times, their flyers, and a random picture of them looking serious behind the decks, then wonder why nobody interacts. That's not how this works. You have to talk to people. Respond to comments. Jump into conversations. Engage with other DJs. The more active you are, the more the algorithm favors you, and the more your audience connects with you.

Stay Ahead of the Trends—But Don't Lose Yourself

Be ahead of the wave, not drowning in it. If there's a viral moment happening, figure out how to remix it into your brand. If people are obsessed with a new sound, be the first to flip it into a set. Don't just follow what's happening—be part of the reason it's happening. But at the same time, make sure your content stays true to your values and doesn't compromise your integrity. Authenticity is what keeps people coming back.

You ever see DJs suddenly jump on a trend that doesn't even fit their style? It looks desperate. Don't be that guy. If it doesn't make sense for your brand, leave it alone. There's a difference between adapting to the moment and completely selling out.

Balance Flexing with Being Human

Nobody wants to follow a walking advertisement. People want to connect with a DJ who feels real. Show them the wins, but also show them the grind. Behind-the-scenes footage, personal insights, even small moments of your daily life—it all adds up to making you relatable. But balance is key. If everything you post is just flexing, you'll push people away. If everything is too casual, you won't be taken seriously. Find the sweet spot.

Let Others Do the Bragging for You

Encourage your fans to share clips, post testimonials, and tag you in their content. A clip of someone saying

"Yo, this DJ just changed my whole night" carries way more weight than you saying "I'm the best." It's about creating moments that people want to talk about.

One trick? Start recording crowd reactions. If you drop a crazy transition and the crowd goes wild, film that moment. That energy speaks louder than any caption you could write.

Your Online Presence is a Business—Treat It Like One

Look at social media like a storefront. If your page looks disorganized, if your videos have terrible lighting, or if your captions are lazy, why would anyone take you seriously? Take the time to clean up your profiles, make your branding consistent, and invest in quality content.

And for the love of music, don't go silent for months. Even if you're not DJing every weekend, stay active. Share throwback clips, make mashups, review new gear, give music tips—keep yourself in the mix. Out of sight, out of mind.

Above All—Be Fearless

Put out content that is useful, entertaining, and completely your own. Let your passion and values drive every post. Be bold. Be different. If you mix on beat, keep your music selection sharp, and respect the craft, the right audience will find you.

Social media is just a tool. It's what you do with it that matters. Play it right, and you won't just be another DJ fighting for attention—you'll be the DJ that people remember, follow, and talk about long after the music stops.

THE FLIP SIDE

Step Back to Move Forward

Sometimes, you need to hit pause. Social media is a powerful tool, but it can also be a bottomless pit of comparisons, distractions, and negativity that drains your energy without you even realizing it. If you're constantly glued to your screen, scrolling through highlight reels of other DJs, you'll burn out faster than a cheap speaker at max volume.

Taking a break isn't a luxury—it's a necessity. When you unplug, you reset. Your mind clears, your focus sharpens, and your creativity has room to breathe. Stepping back from the digital chaos recharges your self-esteem and reminds you why you started DJing in the first place—not for likes, not for clout, but for the love of the music.

Clear the Noise, Elevate Your Game

Without the constant flood of notifications and endless scrolling, your productivity skyrockets. The extra mental space allows you to fine-tune your craft, experiment with new sounds, and create without the pressure of instant validation. That's when the real magic happens. The best ideas don't come when you're obsessing over engagement metrics—they come when you're locked in, fully present, and tapped into your art.

Better sleep, better focus, better music. That's what happens when you cut back on screen time. Instead of frying your brain with blue light at 2 AM, your body syncs back to its natural rhythm. You wake up refreshed, ideas flowing, beats hitting harder, and your overall performance reaching new heights.

Build Real Connections

Social media can trick you into thinking you're networking when you're really just lurking. There's no replacement for real, face-to-face connections. Stepping away from the screen gives you time to hit the gym, meditate, get outside, or dive into activities that keep you sharp and balanced. More importantly, it lets you invest in genuine relationships.

Pull up to events. Shake hands. Meet other DJs, promoters, venue owners, and music lovers in real life. Those moments will do more for your career than any fire post or viral clip ever could. When you're fully present, opportunities find you.

Adapt. Reject. Innovate.

Bruce Lee said it best: *"Adapt what is useful, reject what is useless, and add what is specifically your own."*

Not everything on social media serves you. Some of it inspires, some of it distracts, and some of it straight-up poisons your energy. Know the difference.

So take the damn break. Reset, refocus, and come back stronger. Your creative journey is too important to be drowned out by the digital noise. Sometimes stepping away is the best way to move forward.

PRODUCE MUSIC.

"Fear is only temporary. Regret lasts
forever."
—Unknown

ACT'N A FOOL

Producing is Power

For years, I dodged music production like it was an overdue bill. I let myself believe that DJing alone was enough—that I didn't need to produce tracks or dive into the complexities of sound design. When Ableton, Fruity Loops, and Logic started changing the game, I watched as other DJs seized the moment, crafting their own edits, building their brand, and expanding their reach. And me? I let intimidation and comfort keep me in the same lane.

Looking back, that was a mistake. Producing isn't just a side hustle—it's a gateway to artistic freedom. When you make your own tracks, you're not just playing music, you're shaping the sound of the culture. You're no longer just a DJ—you're a creator.

Don't Just Play the Game—Change It

Think about every legendary DJ who truly made an impact. DJ Premier, A-Trak, Kaytranada, Calvin Harris, Timbaland, Diplo—they didn't just spin records. They crafted sounds. They weren't waiting for the next big track to drop—they were making it themselves.

The reality is, producing opens doors that DJing alone cannot. If you want to secure festival slots, major bookings, and long-term relevance, creating original music is a game-changer. Your own tracks set you apart from every other DJ with a fire playlist.

Fear is the Enemy of Growth

When I finally pushed myself into production, I realized it wasn't as impossible as I made it out to be. I had spent years convincing myself it was too hard, too time-consuming, too complicated. It wasn't. It was just unfamiliar. And that's the real challenge—breaking out of what's comfortable.

If you're feeling that hesitation, fight through it. Start simple. Mess around with loops, build small edits, remix your favorite tracks. Get familiar with the DAW that feels right for you. You don't need to be the next Dr. Dre overnight—just start.

Elevate or Get Left Behind

The music industry moves fast, and DJs who only play other people's music will always be a step behind those who create. You can't afford to sit back and hope for opportunities. You have to build them.

THE BLUEPRINT

DJing is More Than Just Mixing—It's Music Science

DJing isn't just about blending songs together—it's about understanding the DNA of music. You don't need to master every instrument to make a killer remix, but knowing how music works at its core will take you to the next level. The best DJs aren't just selectors—they're creators.

If you want more opportunities, higher pay, and real respect in the industry, you need to start producing your own music. Think of it like training for the big leagues—just like elite athletes study game footage, hit the gym, and refine their technique, DJs must get hands-on with music production. It's a grind, no doubt, but the payoff is massive.

The Right Tools for the Job

Thanks to modern tech, producing has never been easier to access. Whether you're a beginner or looking to level up, there's a DAW (Digital Audio Workstation) for you:

Beginner-Friendly:
 •Serato Studio – Great for DJs transitioning into production.
 •GarageBand – User-friendly and perfect for basic beat-making.

•Logic Pro – A more advanced version of GarageBand but still intuitive.

Pro-Level:
•Ableton Live – A go-to DAW for DJs, known for its looping and live performance capabilities.
•FL Studio (Fruity Loops) – Popular for its easy workflow, used by Metro Boomin, Martin Garrix, and Avicii.
•Pro Tools – The industry standard for professional studio recordings.

Start with what feels right, then expand your skills as you get more comfortable.

Breaking Down the Blueprint

Every genre has a structure, and understanding how tracks are built makes your mixes stronger and your production smoother. Let's break down some of the most common song frameworks:

EDM Structure
•Intro – Sets the mood and builds anticipation.
•Verse – Introduces the melody and sometimes vocals.
•Build-up – Creates tension and energy.
•Drop – The explosive peak where everything collides.
•Breakdown – A breather after the intensity.
•Bridge – A transitional section that keeps things fresh.
•Outro – Closes the journey smoothly.

Hip-Hop Beat Structure
•Intro – A few bars to establish the vibe.
•Verse – The core of the beat, carrying the melody and vocals.
•Chorus – The hook, often the most recognizable and catchy part.
•Bridge – Transitions between sections to switch things up.
•Outro – A clean exit that leaves a lasting impression.

And that's just the tip of the iceberg. Every genre has its own rules—and the best producers learn them, then break them.

Experiment. Evolve. Innovate.

The only way to find your sound is to dive in and experiment. Chop up samples, mess with loops, layer different elements—get your hands dirty. Don't just listen to music—study it. Break down the tracks you love and rebuild them in your own style.

As Albert Einstein once said, *"Creativity is intelligence having fun."*

So get to work. Push boundaries. Break rules. Find your voice. Because the moment you start producing, you're no longer just a DJ—you're a force shaping the future of sound.

THE FLIP SIDE

Collaboration is the Cheat Code

You don't have to be a full-on producer to be a kickass DJ. That's the biggest myth in the game. Some of the most legendary DJs built their careers not by producing beats, but by knowing how to break records, curate energy, and move a crowd.

There are producers out there grinding, cooking up fire remixes, mashups, and exclusive edits—use them. Show love to the remixers, the sound designers, and the underground creators pushing the culture forward. When you spin their work, tag them, and champion their sound, you're not just rocking the decks—you're amplifying the entire DJ ecosystem.

Nobody Cares Who Made the Track—They Care How It Feels

Let's keep it real—most of your audience won't even know if the track you're playing is an original or a remix. They don't care who engineered the kick drum—they care about the vibe. The drop. The moment.

This gives you the ultimate creative freedom. You can flip tracks, experiment with blends, and take risks without getting caught up in the pressure of production. Some DJs treat production like it's a requirement to be respected in the game—but that's bullshit. You can make a full-time living, tour the world, and get booked consistently just by being a master behind the decks.

The Power of Community Over Competition

DJing isn't a solo sport—it's a movement. The more you connect, the more opportunities flow your way. Get to know the remixers, dig through the underground, find the bootlegs nobody else has, and bring something fresh to every set.

When you share the spotlight—when you put other DJs and producers on, support the culture, and uplift your peers—you build a legacy, not just a playlist.

Play the Game Your Way

At the end of the day, your stage presence, track selection, and ability to read a crowd will always be your most valuable assets. Production can be a tool in your arsenal—but it doesn't define your worth as a DJ.

So keep it real. Keep it raw. And most importantly—keep the music alive.

TAP INTO THE COMMUNITY.

"It takes a village to raise a child."
—African proverb

ACT'N A FOOL

Your Talent Alone Won't Get You There—Your Network Will

DJing isn't just about rocking the decks—it's about knowing the right people. You can have the craziest technical skills, the best track selection, and insane stage presence, but if you're not plugged into the right circles, you'll always be a step behind the DJs who are.

I had a friend—an absolute monster behind the decks. He had everything: the skill, the stage presence, the energy. I tried to connect him with a DJ I truly respected, someone who could have put him in the right rooms, introduced him to the right promoters, and maybe even taken his career international.

He refused.

He thought networking was a waste of time, that DJs only looked out for themselves, and that his talent alone would get him where he wanted to be. I get it—most of us DJs are introverts at heart. We love music, we love the craft, but we're not always comfortable with self-promotion or industry politics.

But here's where he messed up.

That same DJ I introduced him to? He later hired multiple DJs to tour internationally with major artists—including me. My boy could have been on that tour, leveling up his career, traveling the world, and making serious money.

But he let his ego and skepticism cost him the opportunity.

The Game Is Built on Relationships

Look, I'm not saying you need to be fake or chase clout—but the reality is, DJs don't just get booked because they're good. They get booked because someone in the right position knows and trusts them. The best gigs don't go to the DJ with the sickest skills; they go to the DJ people feel comfortable working with.

That means you need to:
•Show up. Attend events, even when you're not booked.
•Introduce yourself. A simple, "Yo, I love your work. Let's link up sometime," goes a long way.
•Stay on people's radar. The DJs who stay active in conversations get the calls when opportunities come up.

A Closed Circle is a Career Killer

The DJs who act too cool to network, who isolate themselves, who think their skills alone will make them pop—those are the ones who get left behind. The ones who build real relationships, support their peers, and put themselves in the right spaces? Those are the ones who last in this industry.

So, if you ever get a chance to connect with someone who could change your trajectory, take it. It might just be the move that takes you from local favorite to global headliner.

THE BLUEPRINT

Your Network is Your Net Worth

Navigating the world of DJing can feel like a solo mission—like you're James Bond behind the decks, executing flawless mixes with surgical precision. But even the best agents need allies. Your skills might be top-tier, but if you're out here moving alone, you're making the game harder than it has to be.

Let's keep it real. The DJ community might seem massive, with social media making overnight success look like the norm, but in reality, it's a tight-knit world where everyone talks. The DJs who truly understand the culture know that connections—not just skills—open doors. They're the ones who can introduce you to major gigs, let you test gear that's out of your reach, and challenge your perspective with fresh ideas.

Building Your DJ Circle

So how do you tap into this exclusive network? How do you stop being a lone wolf and start moving like someone who's building a legacy?

First, seek out like-minded DJs who share your passion. Meetup groups, Eventbrite listings, even DJ forums and social media groups are goldmines for finding DJs in your city or niche. If you're serious about leveling up, you need to put yourself in spaces where real DJs talk shop.

Second, don't wait for someone else to make the first move. If you see a DJ crushing a set, introduce yourself. Keep it simple: "Yo, I'm a DJ too. Your set was fire. Let's connect." That's it. No need for a long speech or forced networking tactics. Keep it authentic, and real recognize real.

Third, engage and collaborate. This game isn't just about making friends—it's about creating a circle of trust where you can trade gigs, share advice, and grow together. Think of it like chefs in a top-tier kitchen— when another DJ co-signs your talent, it carries more weight than any flashy promo you can put out.

Expand Beyond Your Comfort Zone

If you're serious about your growth, show up where the real DJs are. Hit up DJ battles, music showcases, and industry conferences like NAMM. If you can't find a meet-up that fits your scene, create your own. Organize a DJ session, a scratch battle, or a music discussion group. Hell, charge a small entry fee while you're at it. Now you're networking and stacking cash.

Why Your DJ Crew Matters

Most partygoers don't know what's happening behind the decks. To them, all DJs look the same. That's why your network of trusted DJs is crucial—they vouch for your skills, recommend you for gigs, and help separate you from the pack. The more DJs and industry professionals co-sign your talent, the stronger your reputation becomes.

At the end of the day, DJing isn't just about playing music—it's about moving in the right circles, building real connections, and making sure your name stays in the right conversations. You never know who's watching, who's recommending you, or what opportunity might come from a simple introduction.

So step out, make that first connection, and get involved. Your career won't build itself—and the DJs who wait for success to come to them are the ones still waiting years later. The ones who put themselves in the mix? They're the ones who win.

Now go get it.

THE FLIP SIDE

The Lone Wolf Advantage: Owning Your Individuality in DJing

For some, flying solo isn't a struggle—it's a superpower. Being a loner as a DJ isn't a disadvantage; it's an opportunity to refine your craft without distractions, to build something that's uniquely yours. When you're not constantly seeking validation or trying to fit into a specific scene, you gain the freedom to experiment, to learn on your own terms, and to carve out a sound and identity that's unmistakably you.

Think of it like being an "orphan DJ"—not in the sense of isolation, but as someone who doesn't follow the pack. You move on instinct, make decisions that serve your artistic vision, and rely on your own creative drive rather than the noise of the crowd. This kind of self-reliance builds confidence, discipline, and originality, three traits that separate the good DJs from the unforgettable ones.

Turning Solitude Into Strength

Being comfortable in your own space gives you a competitive edge. While others are chasing trends or worrying about industry politics, you're honing your skills, sharpening your ear, and developing a signature style that can't be replicated. You don't need a crew to validate you—your work does that for you.

How Going Solo Works to Your Advantage

Independence fuels innovation. When you're not following a trend, you're creating the next one. Solitude allows you to develop a unique sound, something that stands out because it's born from your instincts, not outside influence.

Self-reliance makes you a stronger decision-maker. No second-guessing, no waiting for approval. You trust your gut, and that makes you a more decisive, confident performer.

Personal growth happens in the quiet moments. Without external pressures, you have the space to experiment, study music theory, and perfect your craft without worrying about fitting into a specific lane.

When you do connect with people, it's authentic. Your independence makes you a more valuable collaborator because you bring something real to the table—a perspective and skill set that's been sharpened through dedication, not conformity.

Your Energy Sets the Tone

Flying solo doesn't mean shutting yourself off from the world—it means being fully tuned into yourself. The stronger your sense of identity, the more your music reflects it. The most legendary DJs, the ones who change the game, aren't the ones copying what's already out there. They're the ones who stay true to their vision, even when the world doesn't get it yet.

So, whether you're playing a packed venue or vibing alone in your studio, embrace your individuality. Use it as fuel to create something different, something raw, something undeniably yours.

Because in the end, the DJ who stands alone often stands out the most.

PLAN YOUR WORK, WORK YOUR PLAN.

"A goal without a timeline is just a dream."
—Robert Herjavec

ACT'N A FOOL

The Blueprint for Success: Planning Like a Pro

Every DJ has had that one nightmare gig—the one that still haunts them, years later. For me, it was the time I walked into an event thinking I had everything under control, only to realize I hadn't done my homework. I had been handed a precise setlist, cues, and expectations, but my overconfidence made me skim through it instead of truly locking in. When the solo violinist took the stage, expecting me to have her exact tracks ready, I came up short. I fumbled nearly every cue, and my reputation took a serious hit.

That moment burned a lesson into my brain: Preparation is everything. It's the difference between a flawless, unforgettable set and a sloppy, unprofessional disaster. If you want to run with the best, you've got to plan, strategize, and execute like your career depends on it—because it does.

Mastering the Art of Preparation

Being detail-oriented is what separates an amateur from a pro. The little things—like knowing exactly how much time you have for setup, double-checking your gear, or verifying song versions—can make or break your performance. These aren't just minor details; they're the foundation of a perfect set.

Take the time to review everything before a gig. Don't assume things will just fall into place. Cross-check setlists, confirm special requests, and always, always have a backup plan. When you walk into a venue prepared for every possible outcome, you move with confidence. You're not reacting to chaos—you're controlling the flow.

Why Every Detail Counts

Precision in planning doesn't just make you a better DJ; it sharpens your overall communication skills. When you fully understand what's expected, you can articulate your ideas clearly, whether you're coordinating with a wedding planner, working alongside a live band, or adjusting your set for a last-minute change.

The most successful DJs don't just mix songs—they're masters of execution. They anticipate problems before they happen, adapt to any situation, and maintain complete control over their craft. That's what keeps them booked, respected, and in demand.

Stay Ready So You Never Have to Get Ready

Before every gig, go through your checklist:
 • Verify the details—event time, location, setup, special requests.
 • Triple-check your gear—don't assume everything works. Test it.
 • Communicate—confirm expectations with clients or venue staff.

•Have backups—extra cables, a second USB, and even a backup playlist for emergencies.

It might seem like extra effort, but this is what pros do. Every ounce of preparation boosts your confidence and ensures your audience gets the experience they came for.

You're Only as Good as Your Execution

DJing isn't just about talent—it's about discipline. The DJs who thrive aren't just the most creative; they're the most prepared. Your set should never feel like a gamble. You should walk into every event knowing you're in complete control.

So before your next gig, ask yourself: Are you hoping it goes well, or are you guaranteeing it?

Because the ones who guarantee it—the ones who plan, prepare, and execute with precision—those are the DJs who become legends.

THE BLUEPRINT

The Blueprint: Why Every DJ Needs a Game Plan

A solid timetable isn't just for wedding DJs or corporate event pros—it's a must-have tool for every DJ who takes their craft seriously. Whether you're spinning at a nightclub, festival, private event, or even a pop-up gig, having a clear plan ensures you hit transitions smoothly, keep the energy in check, and deliver a performance that feels effortless.

Think of it as your game plan for the night—the structure that lets you focus on creating moments rather than scrambling to keep up. Without it, you're just hoping things fall into place. Hope is not a strategy.

Pre-Event Planning: Setting Yourself Up for Success

The moment you book a gig, establish a detailed timetable. This isn't just about knowing when to show up —it's about controlling the night before it even begins.

Lock in the schedule, equipment needs, and key players involved. If a client doesn't provide a detailed itinerary, create one yourself. This does two things: it keeps you prepared, and it positions you as the professional who's in control. A DJ who's one step ahead is the DJ that gets called back.

During the Event: Stay Ahead of the Chaos

Even the best-laid plans can shift on the fly. That's why you need to be in constant communication with the host, planner, or event coordinator. Check-in regularly to ensure everything is moving as expected. If things change, adjust smoothly and keep the energy locked in.

Breaking the event into 15-minute intervals helps eliminate guesswork. This method lets you know exactly where the night is going, so instead of reacting, you're orchestrating the experience in real time. When you run a set like this, it's not just a DJ performance—it's a masterclass in crowd control.

The Power of Structure: Order Creates Freedom

Some people think structure limits creativity, but in reality, it's the key to unlocking your best performance. When you work within a tight framework, you can adapt faster, think clearer, and collaborate more effectively. This doesn't just help you—it elevates the entire event.

The audience can feel it when a DJ is in full control. Transitions hit harder, the crowd stays engaged, and even the venue staff syncs up with your rhythm. Everything just flows.

A well-structured timeline isn't about restriction—it's about precision. It allows you to focus on the magic, rather than getting lost in the details. That's what separates a good set from an unforgettable one.

THE FLIP SIDE

Not every gig needs a rigid play-by-play. Some events —like beach parties, rooftop lounges, or laid-back house sessions—are meant to feel organic. Clients might tell you, "We just want a cool vibe, no strict structure." That's your cue to loosen up while still keeping a clear sense of direction.

Even when you're freestyling, your set should still have a beginning, middle, and end. Think of it like storytelling. You wouldn't watch a movie where nothing happens for two hours, so why let your mix feel like it's stuck in one mood all night?

At a chill, casual gig, your job is to curate an atmosphere, not just play songs. This means keeping the energy in waves—maybe starting with laid-back grooves, building up the intensity as the night unfolds, and wrapping things up on a smooth, memorable note.

Master Both Worlds and Elevate Your Game

Knowing when to be strict and when to be flexible is what separates rookies from pros. Some gigs demand pinpoint execution—others require a looser, more instinctive flow. The key is understanding what the event calls for and adapting like a pro.

A DJ who can seamlessly balance structure and spontaneity is unstoppable. You're not just pressing play —you're engineering an experience. That's what keeps crowds locked in and clients calling you back.

So next time you step behind the decks, ask yourself: What kind of ride am I about to take these people on? If you can answer that question with confidence, you've already won the night.

LEARN DJ GEAR, AND ALL TYPES.

"The greatest mastery is mastery of oneself."
—Lao Tzu

ACT'N A FOOL

Every DJ has that one horror story—the gig where things go completely sideways, and you're forced to adapt on the fly. Mine was in New York City, 2011, opening for Funkmaster Flex—one of the biggest opportunities of my career. I was hyped, prepared my set, and brought my USB flash drive like they told me. But when I arrived, I realized something crucial: I didn't fully understand the equipment in front of me.

Instead of the expected laptop hookup, I faced a CDJ setup with a Pioneer DJM900, and my flash drive wasn't formatted properly. No Rekordbox prep, no emergency plan—just me, standing there, completely unprepared. If you've ever felt that "Oh, sh*t" moment before a set, you know exactly what I mean.

Long story short? I couldn't perform. I lost the chance to spin that night, and worse—I never got another shot to work with Flex again.

Prepare for the Unexpected

That night was a brutal lesson, but it changed my entire approach. I spent the next few weeks mastering CDJs, learning Rekordbox, and making sure I could walk into any gig ready for whatever setup was thrown at me. From then on, whether it was Serato, Traktor, CDJs, or even vinyl, I made damn sure I was fluent in every format.

If you're serious about your DJ career, you need to expect the unexpected. You won't always get the ideal setup, and you damn sure won't get time to learn it on the spot. Whether it's a club residency, a corporate gig, or a festival stage, every DJ should know how to:

•Navigate a CDJ setup without a laptop

•Manage a full vinyl setup if needed

•Operate Serato, Rekordbox, and Traktor like second nature

•Adjust to different mixers and controllers without hesitation

You don't need to be an expert in every system, but you must know how to perform under any conditions. Because when you're booked for an important gig, you don't get a second chance to make a first impression.

Test Your Setup Like Your Career Depends on It— Because It Does

There's nothing worse than showing up to a venue, assuming everything is good to go, and realizing your gear won't connect. So make testing your setup a habit. Here's how you avoid the mistakes I made:

•Double-check the venue's equipment BEFORE the gig. If possible, visit the location or get a clear list of their gear.

•Bring backups of EVERYTHING. Spare USBs, cables, dongles, even a backup laptop if you can.

•Test different DJ setups at home or in a studio. Familiarity with different systems means you can adapt under pressure.

•	Format your USB drives correctly and always have Rekordbox-prepped files. CDJs are industry standard—don't assume they'll work like a laptop.
•	Carry your own essentials. External sound cards, power strips, adapters—whatever you might need in a pinch.

When you stay ready, you never have to get ready.

Why Mastering Gear Sets You Apart

The DJs who thrive aren't just the ones with killer track selection—they're the ones who can step into any situation and own it. This is the difference between a DJ who gets gigs occasionally and one who commands the biggest stages consistently.

Being tech-savvy gives you:
•More confidence in high-pressure gigs
•The ability to take last-minute opportunities without fear
•A reputation as a professional who's ALWAYS prepared

Think of it this way: Would you hire a pilot who only knew how to fly one type of plane? Hell no.

The same applies to DJs—be versatile, be prepared, and be unshakable when things don't go as planned.

Because at the end of the day, the DJ who knows their gear inside and out is the DJ who stays booked.

THE BLUEPRINT

Know Your Gear, Elevate Your Performance

As a DJ, you're already handling the heat—reading the crowd, keeping the vibe locked in, and making sure your mixes are tight. But nothing will throw you off faster than technical issues you aren't prepared for. That's why knowing your equipment inside and out isn't optional—it's the difference between a seasoned professional and a DJ scrambling to fix a glitch mid-set.

Your gear is your instrument, and just like any great musician, you need to understand every button, knob, and function to master it. Whether you're rocking CDJs, controllers, turntables, or a hybrid setup, being familiar with your tools means you can troubleshoot, adapt, and execute with confidence—no matter what the night throws at you.

Confidence Comes From Mastery

There's no worse feeling than standing behind the decks, realizing something isn't working, and having no idea how to fix it. Your heart starts pounding, the dance floor starts feeling a little less lively, and suddenly, you're in damage control mode instead of commanding the party.

But when you truly know your gear, you eliminate that fear. Instead of panicking, you problem-solve instantly. Instead of awkward silence, you drop a track with surgical precision. That's the power of being in full control of your setup.

Gear Knowledge = Creative Freedom

The better you know your equipment, the less you think and the more you create. You're no longer second-guessing yourself—you're free to experiment, push boundaries, and craft a set that feels alive.

Mastering your tools allows you to:
•Execute flawless transitions effortlessly
•Manipulate sound in unique ways that elevate your mix
•Layer effects, loops, and samples with precision
•Seamlessly navigate between different genres and tempos

When you're fluent in your gear, you unlock a level of creativity that separates you from the average DJ.

Preparation Is Power

The best DJs aren't just the ones with the hottest track selection—they're the ones who stay ready for anything. Here's how you can make sure you're never caught slipping:
•Read the damn manual. Seriously. Too many DJs rely on trial and error when the answers are right there. Take an hour, sit down, and learn what your gear can actually do.

•Practice in high-pressure situations. Rehearse as if you're already at the gig. Turn off the lights, crank the volume, and simulate the real experience.

•Test different setups. You never know when you'll be forced to use someone else's gear, so familiarize yourself with CDJs, controllers, and mixers outside your usual comfort zone.

•Have a backup plan. Always carry extra USBs, cables, adapters, and even a secondary music source in case something fails.

When you step behind the decks, your only job should be delivering an unforgettable experience. The last thing you want is to be caught off guard by something you could've prepared for.

Your Equipment is Your Weapon—Sharpen It

A great DJ doesn't just press play—they command the room, the sound, and the energy. And that command comes from mastery of the tools at your disposal.

So study your gear, own your craft, and step onto every stage knowing you're ready for whatever comes your way. Because when you're fully prepared, the only thing left to do is blow the crowd away.

A master has failed more times than a beginner has even tried.

Know Your Gear Like You Know Your Setlist

Your equipment isn't just hardware—it's an extension of you. Just like a guitarist knows their fretboard blindfolded or a race car driver feels every turn in the road, a DJ should be able to diagnose a blown speaker by ear, tweak the treble and bass to fit the room instinctively, and know exactly when it's time to upgrade their setup. Mastering your gear isn't just about avoiding technical disasters—it's about elevating your performance and showing your clients you're a true professional.

Would you trust a mechanic who doesn't know their way around an engine? Or an athlete who doesn't understand their own body? Hell no. So why should anyone trust a DJ who doesn't know their own equipment inside and out?

Deep Knowledge Sets You Apart

A true DJ isn't just passionate about playing music—they're obsessed with understanding the craft behind it. You need to be fluent in the language of your gear, from faders and knobs to plug-in ports and level indicators.

But let's be real: you don't need to own every piece of equipment to master it. DJ setups are more similar than you think, so if you don't have high-end gear, go where it is—hit up Guitar Center, test out different controllers, rent equipment, or link up with other DJs who have setups you can learn from.

If you don't have access to certain equipment, YouTube is your best friend. Watch tutorials, take notes, and the moment you get your hands on that gear, start applying what you've learned. The best DJs aren't just the ones with the most expensive setups—they're the ones who know how to make anything work.

Mastering Your Equipment = Next-Level Mixing

Knowing your gear gives you the power to manipulate sound effortlessly. Here's an example:

When I mix, I'll duck the bass on one track and bring in the bassline from the next, making it sound like a brand-new song. When I'm fading out a track, I'll hit the "echo out" function so it vanishes smoothly instead of feeling abrupt.

These are the details that separate good DJs from great ones. And it all comes down to knowing what your tools are capable of.

Learn the Lingo, Own the Game

DJs love to throw around technical terms like they're second nature, and if you don't know what they mean, you're already behind. Here's a quick crash course:
•Sync – Aligns the beats of two tracks for a seamless mix.
•Quantize – Snaps track start and end points to the nearest beat, keeping everything perfectly in time.
•Beat Grid – A visual map of a song's beats, showing where to set cue points, loops, and effects.

On top of that, understanding your waveform colors is a cheat code:

- Red – Low frequencies (bass)
- Green – Mid frequencies (vocals, instruments)
- Blue – High frequencies (hi-hats, treble)

When you pair this with mastery over your hi, mid, and low knobs, you gain total control over how your set sounds. Whether you're layering effects, dialing in a perfect EQ, or adding flanger, echo, or reverb for maximum impact, your technical skills will make you untouchable.

Master the Details, Master the Craft

For DJs, the details make the set. The little things—EQ tweaks, FX layering, beat-matched transitions—are what turn an average DJ into a crowd-controlling monster behind the decks.

So don't just know your music—know your gear like it's second nature. Invest the time, sweat the details, and watch your sets transform from good to legendary.

THE FLIP SIDE

Since new technologies are continuously introduced to the business, it's completely normal for DJs not to know every piece of gear out there. Just take a look at some of the recent innovations—like the cutting-edge Pioneer DJM-V10 and CDJ-3000, which offer integrated streaming, wireless connectivity, and intuitive interfaces. These advancements are exciting, but they serve as tools to enhance your creativity rather than requirements you must master all at once.

You might choose to specialize in a handful of sounds and ideas that you feel most at home with. In fact, focusing on a core set of equipment can actually accelerate your development as a DJ. Remember, trying to master too many new tools can sometimes detract from honing your actual skills. Not every DJ set calls for the most specialized or advanced gear—what matters is using the equipment that works best for you and your listeners.

Whether you're spinning at intimate club nights with a basic setup or commanding huge festival stages with complex rigs, tailor your gear to suit your needs and the vibe you want to create. And as technology continues to evolve, new gear will keep coming out. The key is to stay informed, test new innovations when they make sense for your style, and always focus on how they enhance your performance, rather than getting lost in the hype.

In short, embrace the current breakthroughs like the DJM-V10 and CDJ-3000, but remember: mastery comes from knowing your gear inside and out, not from chasing every new gadget on the market. Keep an eye on what's next, evaluate it based on your personal needs, and let your unique style shine through every set.

TRAIN.

"We do not rise to the level of our
expectations, we fall to the level of our
training."
—Archilochus

ACT'N A FOOL

Like any craft, DJing requires relentless practice and dedication. If you don't put in the time, you will fail—it's that simple. Just ask Desiigner.

In 2016, Desiigner exploded onto the scene with Panda, a track so massive it landed him a deal with Kanye West's G.O.O.D. Music and a #1 spot on the Billboard Hot 100. For a moment, he was everywhere. But after Panda, he struggled to keep his momentum. His follow-ups didn't hit the same, and before long, the industry moved on. Why? Because he relied on hype instead of evolving his craft. Meanwhile, other artists like Travis Scott and Lil Uzi Vert kept refining their sound, staying ahead of trends, and solidifying their place in the game.

The same thing happens to DJs all the time. Some DJs go viral from a single mix or get booked for a big show, then assume that one moment will carry them forever. They stop practicing, stop learning new techniques, and fail to adapt when the industry shifts. The next thing they know, they're being replaced by DJs who did put in the work.

I've seen DJs who killed it in their city, only to bomb when booked for a festival because they never practiced on CDJs. Others lost major gigs because they never mastered transitions, crowd reading, or proper mic work. The difference between a DJ who stays relevant and one who disappears? The work they put in before the gig.

If you want to be more than just a DJ of the moment, you need to constantly refine your skills—experiment with new techniques, stay up to date with evolving gear like the Pioneer OPUS-QUAD or Denon Prime 4+, and master every aspect of your craft.

If you assume talent alone will carry you, you'll end up like Desiigner—someone people remember for one moment instead of a lasting career. Stay sharp, keep pushing, and make sure your name isn't just a trend—it's a legacy.

THE BLUEPRINT

Let's take a moment to appreciate DJ Jazzy Jeff—one of the coldest to ever do it. Back in the 1980s, he started as a bedroom DJ, sharpening his skills in private before the world ever knew his name. Through relentless practice, he transformed himself into a legend, partnering with Will Smith and rocking high-profile events across the globe. His success didn't come from luck—it came from mastery.

And that's the common thread among every DJ who makes it to the top. They obsess over refining their sound, experimenting with new techniques, and constantly pushing their boundaries. You want to be elite? You have to earn it.

Whether you're setting up your first turntable, dialing in your scratching technique, or perfecting the art of seamless transitions, every session adds to your arsenal. Practice isn't just about hitting play—it's about developing the instincts to read the room, control the energy, and pivot on the fly. That's what separates a good DJ from a dangerous one.

Sharpen Your Skill Set Like a Weapon

If you really want to operate like a secret agent behind the decks, here's what you need to lock in:

Master the Art of Blending & Transitions – Beat-matching, looping, effects mixing. Don't just know them, own them. Make transitions so smooth they feel inevitable.

Train Your Ears Like a Sniper Trains Their Shot – Learn to detect micro-changes in sound, recognize instruments instantly, and feel the rhythm like second nature.

Learn Music Theory (Yes, Even for DJs) – You don't need a PhD in it, but understanding scales, chords, rhythm, and harmony will upgrade your sets from good to legendary.

Expand Your Sound Library – The best DJs don't just stick to one genre. Become fluent in house, hip-hop, funk, techno, afrobeats—everything. The more versatile you are, the more untouchable you become.

Invest in Gear That Elevates You – Don't cheap out on your tools. Get quality headphones, turntables, mixers, and controllers. Your sound is your signature—make it crisp.

Build a Network Like a Kingpin – Connections are currency. Collaborate with DJs, producers, and event organizers. The right relationships unlock doors money can't buy.

At the end of the day, greatness isn't gifted—it's engineered. Every mix, every transition, every late night spent perfecting your sound is a deposit into your future success. If you want to move like the greats, train like one.

THE FLIP SIDE

Improvement in any skill doesn't just happen—it's built through intentional effort. While raw talent plays a role, mastery is about refining your abilities through smart, structured learning. You don't have to grind aimlessly for hours, but you do need a game plan to maximize your growth as a DJ.

First, break the process into smaller, digestible pieces. Trying to master everything at once is a recipe for frustration. Instead, focus on key skills one at a time—beatmatching, EQ control, scratching, transitioning. Lock in on each technique until it becomes second nature. Mastery isn't one big leap; it's a series of calculated steps.

Second, absorb as much knowledge as possible. Read, watch, and study everything related to DJing. Learn about different genres, mixing techniques, and the psychology of the crowd. Understanding the "why" behind the music gives you an edge over DJs who just go through the motions.

Third, surround yourself with the right people. No one levels up alone. Finding a mentor or a strong community will accelerate your growth. A seasoned DJ can provide insights you won't find in tutorials, while peers can push you to improve through collaboration and friendly competition.

Now, while structured learning is essential, let's be clear—there's no substitute for practice. Repetition is what transforms knowledge into instinct. The more you mix, the more your brain and body adapt, refining your timing, transitions, and crowd control. It's like building muscle: the more you train, the stronger you get.

If you want to be great at anything, especially DJing, you have to put in the hours. There's no shortcut to experience, but there are ways to make every session count. Study, strategize, and practice with intent, and soon enough, you won't just be playing music—you'll be commanding the crowd with precision.

CONCLUSION

Final Words: The Art of the DJ

What you put into your life is what you get out; it's about proper exchange. Everything we've covered in this book will make you a better musician, but the only way to truly succeed is by putting in the work. There are no shortcuts, no instant fame, no overnight success stories that last. The greatest DJs—the ones who leave their mark—understand that this journey takes time. Days, weeks, months, years.

That's what being a great DJ is all about. Constant growth. It's about mastering the fundamentals, then pushing beyond them. It's about reading the room like a poker player, staying five steps ahead, controlling the energy, and setting the tone for the night. It's about understanding rhythm, not just in music, but in life.

A great DJ knows how to use their voice as an instrument, whether it's hyping a crowd, guiding a moment, or simply knowing when to let the music speak for itself. They know the power of staying present and paying attention—to the crowd, to the mix, to the energy in the room. They love themselves enough to stand firm in their artistry while staying humble and accountable enough to keep learning.

This isn't just about music. It's about courage. The courage to put yourself out there, to experiment, to fail, to try again. It's about having the bravery to be different, the confidence to create something new, the humility to accept criticism, and the discipline to get better every single day. It's about knowing when to seek help, whether from mentors, peers, or the countless resources available to you. It's about staying curious, never settling, and constantly asking: What's next?

And most of all, it's about consistent training.

You've seen it in every story, every lesson in this book—the DJs who last, the ones who make real waves, are the ones who never stop refining their craft.

If you mix on beat, keep an eclectic music library, and treat people with respect, you will find success. Whether your goal is to rock weddings, command nightclub stages, build an international brand, or simply throw the dopest house parties, the blueprint is the same: Master your skills, respect the craft, and always evolve.

At the end of the day, there is a beat inside of you waiting to come out and play. You don't need permission to be great. You just need the dedication to keep going.

So go. Be fierce. Be confident. Be relentless. The world is waiting to hear your sound.

It's on you now, DJ.

www.ingramcontent.com/pod-product-compliance
Lightning Source LLC
Chambersburg PA
CBHW081132090426
42737CB00018B/3309